"The scenery is altogether sublime beyond description"

. New Island, West Falkland . October 29, 1820 . Captain Macy, Brig *Aurora*, New York .

. Right . *The stillness of the water's surface mirrors the late afternoon landscape, New Island, West Falkland .*

Ian Strange & Georgina Strange

Design In Nature

Falkland Islands Landscapes

Atmosphere

. Published by . Design In Nature .

. Authors & Photographers . Ian J Strange MBE & Georgina Strange .

. © 2005 Design In Nature .

. www.designinnature.com .

. Log Book quotes © Nantucket Historical Society .

. Printed by . Butler & Tanner Ltd., England .

. First Published 2005 .

ISBN 0-9550708-0-5

DESIGN IN NATURE

. Right . Early morning sea mist envelopes Beef and Coffin Islands, West Falkland .

Introduction

'A t m o s p h e r e' presents a series of images of the Falkland Islands not often portrayed. A unique feature of these Islands is their quickly changing weather patterns, bringing a beauty to these often remote and little known landscapes that are rare in many other parts of the world.

Consisting of two main islands, East and West Falkland, and some 420 smaller islands and islets, the Falklands are set deep in the South Atlantic. Lying approximately 280 miles NE of Cape Horn and the tip of South America, they present a fascinating contrast to this neighbouring continent. The Islands' environment is unique, from its landscapes portrayed here, its wildlife and untouched nature, to its peoples and their very English way of life.

This collection of photographs by Design In Nature show many areas of the Falkland archipelago. These images attempt to illustrate, not only the changing atmosphere of these Islands, but the variety of beautiful landscapes that are a dominant feature of the Falkland Islands. Text is purposely limited to captions and a few anecdotal writings, the intention being that the photographs speak for themselves.

. Main Image . Stone Runs near Estancia, East Falkland .
. Above . Scurvy Grass in flower & the berries of the native Diddle Dee (Empetrum rubrum) .

Many of the images and the atmosphere they portray are timeless and in this respect these relatively modern photographs of the Falklands landscape probably show little change from the time man first set foot ashore on the Islands. Each image has a memory for the photographers and in some cases these are noted in the text. In a few cases throughout the book, dates are given of when a particular photograph was taken, so that hopefully sometime in the future they may be used as important references.

Equally important were the descriptions written of these landscapes by much earlier intruders into this wilderness, therefore it was felt fitting that the writings of some of these early whalers accompanied certain images.

Charles Darwin made two relatively short visits to the Falkland Islands, both confined to the east of East Falkland. Describing these landscapes he wrote of their extreme desolation, dreary nature and uniformity of their brown colour. His portrayal of these Islands has been bestowed on us for over 100 years. How very wrong Darwin was in his descriptions.

We hope that this work will go some way to show these Islands in their true beauty.

. Right . A winding pathway through the Sand Grass leads to Surf Bay, East Falkland .

Design In Nature

These images are presented by the father and daughter team, Ian & Georgina Strange who work under the title of Design In Nature. Our work is almost entirely devoted to aspects of nature, attempting to show the beautiful forms, design and colour to be found in nature's own environment, hence the title of our studio.

The photographs exhibited within the covers of this work have been selected from a large file of images of the Falkland Islands. These have been gathered, at least by one member of the team, during some forty years of photography. The problem was not so much what to put into this work, but what had to be left out.

Defining the term "atmosphere" was one that had to be wrestled with. Images of misty landscapes, rough seas and low evening light was the original direction, but equally important, there was a need to show the incredible clarity, calmness and warmth that also features in these unique Islands.

No apologies are made for the number of photographs depicting New Island, lying on the extreme west of West Falkland. This island is exceptional for its scenery and nature, but it is also our home. Obtaining pleasing images, especially atmospheric landscape images, requires that element of luck, but this increases when you are able to understand from experience, some of the intricate patterns of a specific environment and its weather. For us, that specific environment is New Island, but even then, a wait in anticipation of a scene developing into a preferred image can often be in vain.

We continue to use conventional photographic equipment for all of our work, and all of the images in this book were taken on either a Rolleiflex 6x6, Leica, or Canon 35mm camera. Fujifilm Provia 100F provides a perfect rendition of the colours of the Islands' landscape, and there is no need for the use of enhancing filters when nature provides such a spectacular show for free!

There is an element of frustration in using conventional equipment, in that working in such a remote part of the globe, colour film has to be sent elsewhere for processing. However, the compensation is being able to handle negatives and transparencies which we still believe have the edge over digital images, particularly for this genre of photography. However, at the end of the day we strive for the very best in our photographs and will follow whichever technical course will help us achieve that.

We hope that apart from a collection of pleasing images, you find *Atmosphere* informative, as well as a valuable record of some of the most beautiful and remote areas of the Falklands; one of the precious remaining unspoilt areas of wilderness in the World.

. Right . The northern shoreline of Cape Pembroke, East Falkland .

. Left . Surf Bay sand dunes, East Falkland .
. This page . Dusk falls over the hilltops of New Island, West Falkland .

"*First part calm, mid part a light breeze from NNW, course E. Latter part fresh breezes, at 3pm made the Jason Islands. Bearing NE at 4 braced the yards and brought the ship to the wind, at sunset tacked ship and stood off the land and took in sail.*" . Jason Islands, February 1, 1833 . Richard Luce, Master . Whaler Condor, Fairhaven .

. *Right . Evening light over Steeple Jason Island from the summit of Grand Jason Island, West Falkland . 1986 .*

The remote Jason Island group in the North West corner of the Falklands archipelago holds striking scenery and an abundance of wildlife

. Main Image . A View to Carcass and West Point Islands from South Jason Island, 1983 .
Above . Striated Caracara roosting at sunset on Elephant Jason Island, & the rugged coastline of Steeple Jason Island
from the air .

"At 11am we anchored at Elephant Jason Island,
at 3pm had got blubber of 40 elephants on board
and what few skins they had got. Prime fur seal
skins 225, fur pup skins 416, elephant 41."

. Elephant Jason Island, West Falkland, January 13, 1817 . Paul West, Master, Ship *Cyrus*, London .

. Main Image . Elephant Jason Island, West Falkland . Despite depredations by early sealers, the Jason Islands
remain valuable reserves for different species of seal.
. Below . Yellow Daisy (Senecio littoralis) amongst lichen covered quartzite . Feldmark type vegetation of cushion plants
and tussac grass cover large areas of Elephant Jason Island .

. The idyllic South End Beach on New Island, West Falkland .

" *This day commences with strong SW gales and squally. Employed in stowing down and landing casks... on Peat Island.* "

. New Island, West Falkland . April 3, 1839 . Captain
Benjamin S. Cutler, Schooner *Bolton*, Stonington .

. Left . A storm clears over Peat Island . New Island, West Falkland .
. Right . Sunlight through storm clouds illuminates the bay where the
Glengowan lies shipwrecked, New Island .

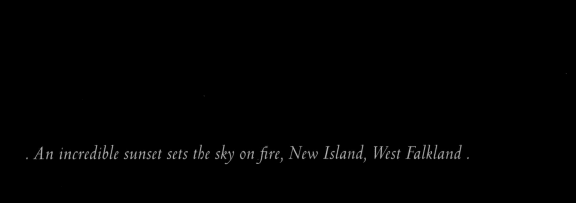

. *An incredible sunset sets the sky on fire, New Island, West Falkland .*

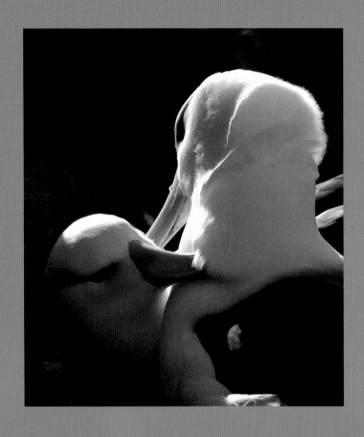

"Saw Buchêans Island bearing SE by E 3 leagues distant, at 3pm calm and good weather, at 4pm sprang up a fresh breeze at SW and at 6 landed a crew for ceiling on Buchêans Island. Ends with strong winds at SW and hazy weather"

. Beauchêne Island . December 11, 1817 . Edmund Fanning, Master, Sloop Magellan .

. Right . The Anvil Stack on Beauchêne Island in the South East of the Falklands . This remote island and its formidable coastline is often pounded by rough seas. The island is a closed nature reserve and site of one of the largest colonies of Black-browed Albatross in the Falkland Islands.

. Above . A pair of Black-browed Albatross preening each other in a courtship display .

. Early morning and the sky above the main colony on Beauchêne Island is already filled with Black-browed Albatross .

. Beauchêne Island's East side, looking south to the Citadel . October 1983 .

. Beauchêne Island's west side & the main Black-browed Albatross colony .

"At 1pm sent a boat ashore at Beauchênes for fish or whatever else they could obtain. Lay off and on.
At 3pm saw a sail in SW steering for island. At 5pm the boat returned bringing some seal skins and penguins.
Could not get any fish."

. Beauchêne Island . January 19, 1848 . Benjamin C. Sayer, Master, *Edmund Cary* . Nantucket .

"On the west side of the island one of the largest

Black-browed Albatross and Rockhopper penguin colonies

I had seen. Such an island had to qualify as a very valuable

reserve."

. Beauchêne Island . Author's note book entry . November 1965 .

. *Right . Illuminated by the sun, the Port San Carlos River snakes through the landscape of East Falkland .*

. Left . Loch Head Pond House in late evening light,
East Falkland . 1981 .

. Right . Early morning autumn sunlight through stratus clouds
casts a hazy glow over the bay, New Island, West Falkland .
. Sunlight illuminates the surface of the sea like
liquid silver, Sea Lion Island .
Early morning & clearing storm clouds,
New Island, West Falkland .

. Left . Snow squalls over the east coast of East Falkland .
. Right . Foul Bay at Cape Dolphin, East Falkland .

. Cumulus clouds rise over West Falkland behind the old sheep pens on Weddell Island .

Early morning Stratus lies over the hills behind the shearing shed, Carcass Island, West Falkland . 1984 .

"Fair weather and moderate breeze. At 3pm hove up anchor, made sail and ran into the great West Point harbour and at 4.30pm came to anchor in five and a half fathoms. A fine white sandy bottom. Went on shore on the English Malone to hunt."

. Hope Harbour, West Falkland . December 3, 1817 . Whaler *Sea Fox* . New York .

. *Right* . *Penguin Point Bay, Hope Harbour, West Falkland .1969 .*

Left . The view over Ten Shilling Bay at Port Stephens, West Falkland .

. Right . Wave cloud over the Mount Robinson ranges
on the West Falkland mainland .
. Whaler Bay, Roy Cove, coloured rusty red by Sorrel
in the late summer light . 1965.
. Winter light over the Weddell Island group, West Falkland .

. The sun sets in a blaze of gold over the sea . New Island, West Falkland .

. The view across Byron Sound from Hill Cove Settlement, West Falkland .

. Horses & the view to Mt. Tumbledown & The Two Sisters, Stanley, East Falkland .

. *A double rainbow over the colourful roofs of Stanley, East Falkland* .

During winter, the quality of the light & the spectacular sunsets make for excellent atmospheric photo opportunities, and when the snow does fall, the landscape is transformed...

Tempered by its marine environment, the Falkland Islands have a narrow temperature range. Contrary to general belief, accumulations of snow are rare. In the mid winter months of June and July, the ground rarely freezes and the average temperatures are around 7 °C

. Left . Mid-winter near Stanley, East Falkland .

.Right . The silhouette of rooftops in Stanley under a misty haze .
. A stunning winter sunset in Stanley .
. Snow-capped mountains from the air, East Falkland .

. *Mount Pleasant Road in mid-winter after heavy snow, East Falkland* .

. *Mid-winter snow falls over Surf Bay in the late afternoon light, East Falkland* .

The Black Tarn, a glacially eroded corrie, & the summit of the highest peak on the East Falkland mainland, Mt Usborne

. Above . Mount Usborne & the Black Tarn .
Amongst the most striking landscapes of the Islands are the accumulations of grey quartzite blocks
or boulders known as 'Stone Runs' or 'Rivers of Stone' .
. Left . The bright red berries of Diddle Dee and the Feugian Tall Fern add a splash of vibrance to the landscape .

. Left . Shag Cove & Falkland Sound glow in the early morning
light, West Falkland . 1969 .
. Right . Wine Glass Bay, Port Louis camp on the north coast of
East Falkland .

. Main image . Stormy skies clear to the east over New Island .
. Right . Winter sunrise over Cliff Knob Island .

"The first part brisk wind at NNE. At 4 this morning we
wade anchor and came out and run SW. We left New Islands
at 11 clock and very thick rainy weather and brisk wind at
N by E. So ends the day."

. New Island . January 22, 1792 . George Bunker, Master, Ship *Washington* . Whaling voyage out of Nantucket .

. *Early morning light & Cumulus clouds rising behind Coffin and Beef Islands . New Island, West Falkland .*

. Gorse in full flower & smmer rain squalls over Weddell Island . New Island .

Almost at every moment of the day the scene is continually changing its atmosphere and mood

The ever-changing colours in the sky are a source of constant
fascination, & the Falkland Islands offer some of the most stunning
to be found anywhere

. Left . A hazy start to the day over Cliff Knob & Beef Islands,
New Island, West Falkland .
. Right . A crimson sunrise over the bay & the wreck of the
Glengowan, New Island .
. The same view as above, on a different morning shows
the islands in a contrasting light .

"*Viewed many of the wonders of nature in the perpendicular
cliffs which bound the seaboard sides of this island.
The whole content of the outer shore is composed of rocks
arranged in regular strata,
intersected by perpendicular seams which give the whole
the appearance of an artificial structure.*"

. New Island, West Falkland . October 29, 1820 . Captain Macy, Brig *Aurora* . New York .

. Left . The striking sea cliffs of New Island's west side in a 50 knot gale .

. Left . South Fur Island, Jason Island group, West Falkland .
The only island of its kind in the archipelago, being composed
entirely of blocks of dolerite . 1984 .
. Right . Storm Beach boulders with algae . Flat Jason Island,
West Falkland .

. *Bird Island, with a view to the West Falkland mainland* .

. Sea cliffs on the south west side of Bird Island .1986 .

"Very cold with showers for the third day. Overcast with strong 35 knot plus winds from the SSW. Heavy seas pounding the island with spray going up and over the Citadel Bluff."

. Beauchêne Island . Author's note book entry . December 1, 1983 .

. Left . Beauchêne Island & the Anvil Stack under heavy rain clouds .
. Below . Rockhopper penguins arriving from feeding at sea, & late evening sunlight on the ocean .

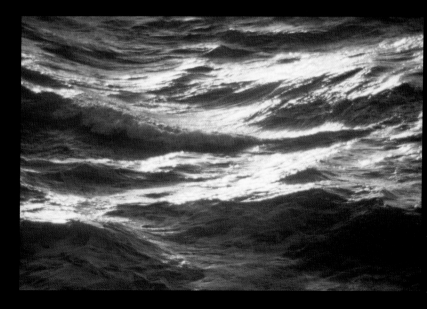

. Left . The unique structure of Blinn's Stack, Beauchêne Island .

This page . Rockhopper Penguins coming ashore in rough seas on Beauchêne Island .

Our Thanks

The images shown in this work have been taken over a period of some forty years and during that time a very large number of people have been directly or indirectly involved.

One of the earliest photographs in this work goes back to the autumn of 1965. On the back of a tractor drawn trailer, a very bumpy ride was endured from Roy Cove to Whaler Bay to recover the remains of a rare form of beaked whale. While there I photographed the falling light on a scene in this area and the result is shown in this book. For this I have the late Jack McCallum to thank, as he was my guide and the driver of that tractor.

In slightly more modern times with somewhat more sophisticated transport, the image of "Wave Clouds over the Mount Robinson Range on West Falkland" was by courtesy of the crew of an RAF Chinook helicopter. Perhaps because we were already flying at a fairly high altitude in exceptional weather, the decision was taken to try and break an altitude record for this particular type of helicopter. From the side door of the Chinook I captured the scene during our ascent, if I remember correctly at several thousand feet. Unfortunately, but perhaps also prudent in these circumstances, I do not recall the names of the crew, but have them to thank for this image.

There were many instances like the above, either people who helped, usually with transport, or many more who gave us the opportunity and permission to enter their lands and take these images. To all these individuals past and present we extend a big thank you.

The collecting together of photographs is only part of the work, behind the scenes so to speak were those who gave technical advice and/or constructive criticism such as Dan Birch, the printing firm Butler & Tanner, Nikki Buxton of Synergy Information Systems and especially Mick Carter.

. Left . Cape Pembroke & the lighthouse, near Stanley, East Falkland .

The inclusion of writings from old log books comes from another project, but without the help of Betsy Tyler of Nantucket and the kind permission of the Nantucket Historical Association, they would not have emerged.

A turn of events, especially for the younger member of the team, leads us to extend thanks to the Falkland Islands Government. They sponsored her university training in Australia, where a degree in photography and related subjects such as publishing was gained.

We thank John Young of the Geoffrey C Hughes Trust, who in an indirect way played an important part by supporting our background work on New Island.

Last but not least Maria is especially thanked for the part she played in the production of this work.

Finally we dedicate this work to the continuation of New Island as a reserve in perpetuity, and its protection under the New Island South Conservation Trust.

Ian J. Strange MBE & Georgina Strange

Design In Nature
New Island House
Stanley
Falkland Islands

Atmosphere

. New Island, West Falkland . February 1, 1786 . Captain William Mooers, Ship *Maria* . London

"This morning fine weather, wind at WNW so the latter part we returned of our voyage, got plenty of geese and fur seal. So ends this day."